A LONG TIME LEAVING

Beirut Journal

CAROL A. HAYES

Copyright © 2024 Carol A. Hayes.

All rights reserved. No part of this book may be used or reproduced by any means, graphic, electronic, or mechanical, including photocopying, recording, taping or by any information storage retrieval system without the written permission of the author except in the case of brief quotations embodied in critical articles and reviews.

LifeRich Publishing is a registered trademark of
The Reader's Digest Association, Inc.

LifeRich Publishing books may be ordered
through booksellers or by contacting:

LifeRich Publishing
1663 Liberty Drive
Bloomington, IN 47403
www.liferichpublishing.com
844-686-9607

Because of the dynamic nature of the Internet, any web addresses or links contained in this book may have changed since publication and may no longer be valid. The views expressed in this work are solely those of the author and do not necessarily reflect the views of the publisher, and the publisher hereby disclaims any responsibility for them.

Any people depicted in stock imagery provided by Getty Images are models, and such images are being used for illustrative purposes only. Certain stock imagery © Getty Images.

ISBN: 978-1-4897-5108-9 (sc)
ISBN: 978-1-4897-5107-2 (e)

Print information available on the last page.

LifeRich Publishing rev. date: 10/16/2024

PREFACE

Because this work began as a Journal, I kept it in that form throughout. Its entries were made on days and nights that had a special effect on me, and as a result, it does not read like a story. It is a succession of events. It is the emotions and fears and happenings of six years in a foreign country that was either in the throes of, or the aftermath of war. It is not a work to enjoy, but it is an honest account that is often painful and sad. It is a glimpse of mankind in all his dangerous blundering and his endless struggle to survive his own mistakes.

DEDICATION

This work is dedicated to my daughters who through their very existence saved me.

Also dedicated to my husband of 17 years who long ago put his hand out to me and saved me from the shadows of another life. Without his help, this journal would not have been edited or formatted.

Carol A. Hayes

INTRODUCTION

Current Day: It's early. The house is night - dark and quiet. My cats slumber in postures of comfort around the room. Moonlight graces a corner of the oriental carpet, causing the reds and blues to glow in ghostly shades. A small streak of moonlight travels across my chair and down the other side. My life is peaceful now and good. Yet, on sensual nights such as this my mind returns to that part of me that lived another life entirely.

1972: In my early days of college, I met a handsome and intelligent man from the country of Lebanon. His exotic allure was such a contrast to my quiet rural upbringing that it was hard to resist the pull of adventure and an ancient culture. Our romance was heady and wonderful, and in six short months we married. That same year war broke out in Lebanon. War was something I had no experience with, and as it was far away, it did not affect me. Little did I know how it would change my life forever.

Time passed rapidly, filled with love and flight school, and after four years my husband completed his studies. A pilot job in Lebanon was offered working with Lebanon's cargo airline, and we prepared to leave. The goodbyes to my family and gentle way of life were gut-wrenching, yet on a different level I was exhilarated. The magic carpet carried us on our way, and as we went, I tried to prepare myself for a different way of life. My husband would be going home to all that was familiar, while I would need to absorb a new country, a difficult language, a close-knit family and the threat of war.

We traveled from Portland, Oregon to Seattle, Washington, to London, England. From London we flew to the island of Cyprus in the Mediterranean. Larnaca, Cyprus was a layover destination before the last leg of our journey into Lebanon.

Cyprus was captivating! Flowers danced in enormous overflowing pots around the hotel, palm trees lined the drive. The ancient streets, narrow and worn, twisted through the town, each with a beguiling glimpse of blue sea at its end. The streets culminated at a picturesque promenade along the harbor, complete with gently bobbing boats and open-air restaurants, The sea spoke to me throughout the day and night. Moonlight lay across its gentle breast. Perfection surrounded me in the balmy nights. It was my own private taste of an incredibly romantic way of life.

PROPHECY

*Sea song
through the open window
moon on the ocean's face.
We lie together
light and dark,
replete and quiet;
a timeless moment
in a timeless land.
The forever of it soothes me,
even as our moment passes
into the night-time sea.*

Part I

INITIATION

January 1977 to February 1977

January 1977

Journal Entry

We left Cyprus for Lebanon on a Wednesday at 5 PM. The small airport was busy, full of vacationing Lebanese eager to return home. I was very nervous. All too soon the call to board came, and we were on our way. The flight, once airborne, took a mere twenty minutes. The plane banked toward the land mass of Lebanon, swooping down low over the Mediterranean, to circle over the city of Beirut. Sunset flashed here and there from many windows below, with a cheerful ruddy color that spoke of the passing of a warm and lovely day. As the plane descended the more obvious it became that all was not well in Beirut. Windows that had just a moment ago glowed so warmly, now looked like broken teeth in a devastated face. Sunset was soon replaced by a brooding half-light, and as the plane landed the city was swallowed up in darkness. We rolled to a stop before the terminal and a squeaking, lumbering stair bumped up against the plane. Stepping down onto the tarmac, we threaded our way through great holes in the pavement to the terminal. Generators rumbled. Khaki-clad soldiers with machine guns watched us as we passed.

Propane lamps lit the terminal with a harsh white light, as there was no electricity. The area was dirty and very crowded, night air came in through broken windows. Soldiers with guns patrolled the dusty floor.

The line was long at the passport check. My passport and visa were carefully scrutinized, and the questions were fired at me in a language that I did not understand. My husband began to wave at someone in the crowd, and suddenly his father stood before us. He shook my hand to welcome me. Family surrounded us, all talking at once, in beautiful but as yet unintelligible Arabic. My husband's mother eyed me with doubt, unsure as to whether I was deserving of her son. I silently vowed to prove myself to her.

The trip from the airport was tortuous, down streets devoid of light and cluttered with rubble and garbage. Many times, we swerved violently to avoid a shell hole or collapsed wall. Beams from the headlights rebounded strangely from the looming bulk of eyeless buildings. Nothing seemed to exist beyond those wavering spheres of light, and the journey became somewhat dream-like.

After many twists and turns, one of the blind structures became important. The car halted in front of its vague outline, and we clambered out. The darkness of the street flowed into the foyer of the building as we entered. It was black and thick with a humid cloying texture that pressed against my eyes. I felt completely blind, and afraid to take a step. Soon a lighter flared and a candle was lit. We struggled up the stairs with our baggage, while shadows played grotesquely across the marble walls and floors. Voices echoed strangely in the chill dark.

Suddenly a door opened on the landing above us and warm light and sound pushed through the dark and spilled down the stairs into our faces. There was laughter and confusion as the rest of the family surrounded us. I was struck with the contrast between the darkness we had just emerged from, and the warmth and light of the family.

Journal Entry

Our first night here was filled with explosions and the loudest thunder I have ever heard. I sleep little.

Journal Entry

Today we went for a "tour" of the city, passing many checkpoints where we were to stop and have the car searched for weapons. We drove through parts of the once prosperous city where most of the buildings are gutted by fire, while others are completely collapsed. Such ancient buildings now useless, many lives wasted, a proud heritage abused.

Journal Entry

The Koran is chanted over a loudspeaker, a man across the street has died. His coffin is carried to his home in a beat-up station wagon with no windows, then into his house where the family will watch over his body for one day, then bury him. For seven days they will mourn his passing. It seems sadly ironic that he survived the war to succumb to a heart attack afterward. He was 47

Journal Entry

Today a man was killed because he passed two guard posts without stopping. The Syrians asked no questions and shot him dead. We watched them take his body from a Syrian truck and place it in an ambulance that drove slowly away.

Across the street from here is a Syrian outpost. The men stand ready with their machine guns. Sometimes in the night I hear the spatter of guns and I think about the tanks along the streets buried to ground level like crouching predators. The Middle East has taught me as I would never have been taught elsewhere that life is precious, fragile, and short; yet it is perpetual. Here people die proudly with curses of hate and breaths of love on their lips.

Journal Entry

Another tour through the center of town, waiting in traffic jams caused by the lack of traffic lights and the inevitable search for weapons and identification papers by the Syrians.

Along the way I saw shopkeepers in stalls made from scrap, selling anything they can; fruit, fish, vegetables. On the coast road there are shops that sell stolen furniture, Persian carpets and other housewares, looted from the Christian side. Farther along the coast we passed the marina with its shells of burned-out boats.

We travelled along avenues of broken and dying palm trees, past mountain after mountain of garbage and the hulks of rusted, smashed cars. In the city again we passed many places where fighting was exceptionally fierce, and in front of a Muslim orphanage there were machine gun holes in the wall where children were wounded and scared to death because they were of the wrong religion. Later we came to a park of graceful cedars, many acres long now converted into a cemetery filled with the bodies of those who died. In some places there are large fenced areas where many people are buried en masse; unknown forever. Along the walls of buildings there are pictures of those who died and those missing; many of them are children. I am sure that there is too much hate here and everywhere for there ever to be true peace, I believe the world will come to a violent end through some holocaust to rid it of man's desire to inflict agony on his brothers.

Journal Entry

It has been very cold. We sit huddled around a charcoal fire as there is no other heat. The electricity is sporadic and goes off at the most inconvenient times. Many times there is no hot water and we all forgo showers and wash in cold water, very quickly.

Journal Entry

Today we go to the American University to meet an American professor and his wife. They have lived in Beirut for 12 years and learned no Arabic due to their isolation in an island of Americans. As we walked through the main gates, I immediately felt like I was back in the States. Everything was tidy, no litter, no garbage mountains. Their apartment was lovely with a view of the sea; it was so warm inside and had hot water. I longed to stay there where it wasn't cold and luxuriate in a warm shower. But, all too soon we took leave of their hospitality and walked back into the harsh world of the Lebanese.

It is very difficult to be comfortable here but something about the tenacity of the people causes me to respect them as they pick up the pieces and make their shops and homes from nothing. The picture of the downtown is a mixture of piles of scrap and bright shops. Somewhere there is someone crying, someone laughing, someone starving, somewhere someone becoming rich on other people's misfortunes.

Journal Entry

Tonight, we walked along the street being careful not step inadvertently in an open manhole or sewer. As we walked, many Syrian tanks passed loaded down with helmeted men and bristling with guns. Something is brewing in the south on the Israeli border.

The view from my window is a street full of holes from bombs, one in the middle of the street marks the spot where a woman was killed while walking arm in arm with her daughter. The girl was unharmed, At the end of the street is a Christian Church. All the windows of stained glass are broken and the cross at the top is cleaved into a two-pronged devil's staff by a sniper's bullet.

Journal Entry

My husband is away again, my brother-in-law takes me to the American University Hospital today about an ear problem. There are very few doctors, all the waiting rooms are full, people are sleeping on the floor. I am rather relieved that no doctor was available, because the place is filthy, with cockroaches and garbage. Infection is rampant. We then drive to the old part of the city, the part that is absolutely ancient. Every building is in ruins, the winding streets so choked with junk we can barely drive through. As we wind our way through the buildings the light flickers through the shell holes. All the buildings are a total loss. We pass the remains of a theater, its marquee still displaying the movie title "The Longest Day". On the way home solders stop the car and tell us to get out. They search the driver, then the car and tell us to go on.

Journal Entry

We drove along the coast road south to Sidon today. Along the way there are many villages all touched by the war. Many villas are burned out and vacant. Once fashionable hotels are now homes for refugees. Laundry hangs from every window. When we returned home, we found the electricity off and several people trapped in the elevator.

Journal Entry

My husband has been assigned a temporary base in Tokyo, Japan After much planning, it has been arranged to leave tonight. This afternoon, bombs are falling and guns are firing. I wonder if it will keep us from leaving. I have felt so desolate and depressed. I wonder how people keep going. I think I am pregnant.

Part II

THE DAILY STRUGGLE

October 1977 to June 1981

Journal Entry

It is October now and we are on the way back to Beirut. Coming with us is our new daughter who is less than one month old. As we come in over the city, I think how much the same it looks and wonder what it will be like this time. It is our final destination. I must try to make it a home. We are met at the airport as before; we are taken home and warmly greeted by all. They are enchanted by the baby, and it makes me feel less strange.

Journal Entry

It is cold, the heat and electricity are still sporadic. There is hot water only twice a day. I go through the same culture shock as before, loneliness, anger, frustration, self-persecution. I feel insulted because my mother-in-law bathes the baby. I think she believes I am not capable. It's hard to know because I cannot talk with her.

Journal Entry

We are finally in our own apartment in the same building as the in-laws. Still the lack of aloneness depresses me. These people are so family oriented, so interested being together for entertainment and support, that I find my independence out of place, gradually I relax and begin to blend in and stumble along with the language. When guests come, we are the topic of conversation. They wonder if I know how to cook, or if I am a good mother.

Journal Entry

There is still garbage everywhere, it will take years to re-educate the people into picking up litter. They are beginning at least, and when I see a store merchant sweeping up around his shop, I applaud him silently from my balcony.

Journal Entry

The weather is getting warmer now, and I am beginning to feel the same slowness creeping on me as I did in Cyprus. I believe it's the Mediterranean climate.

Journal Entry

There is a disturbing custom here since the war, that on special holidays such as New Years, people shoot their machine guns in the air. This same activity also follows births, weddings, funerals and general well-being or the opposite. One New Years Day I found a bullet that had stopped short four inches from our verandah door.

Journal Entry

It is so interesting to watch from my window and see the people going places, men selling their wares, mostly on foot or in any conveyance possible, some with carts, others with donkeys and horses. Every morning, I hear the women beating their carpets with a vengeance that is evidently a method of self-expression. Laundry hangs over the street in its myriad colors, the flags of every household; they drip down upon the passerby. Most clothes are washed by hand.

The butcher across the street has two sheep tied up by his shop every Monday, and he butchers them on the sidewalk. All the little boys come and watch, the remaining sheep watches too, and I can see the knowledge in its eyes. I cannot watch. Below our apartment is a small grocery owned by a man named Fohad. All the women of the surrounding buildings at various times of the day, call his name from their balconies. until they are recognized by him, at which time they send down a basket on a rope with their list inside. Fohad fills the order, tugs on the rope, and up goes the basket, speedy home delivery.

Journal Entry

All is rather peaceful, and I forget where I am and what has happened here, and I begin to feel comfortable.

Journal Entry

One evening as we sat with the family, we heard the sound of planes, and I am told it was an air raid from Israel. We all take cover in the entry way away from windows, that are partially left open to prevent shattering. My heart has stopped. I listen dumbly to the bombs fall and wonder what I am doing here.

Journal Entry

This morning, we drove toward Sidon and Tyre where the Israelis are taking over sections of the south of Lebanon. All along the way there are soldiers with guns. We are turned back by a roadblock ten kilometers from the front line. When we returned, we passed two bombed cars that had held twelve women and children escaping from the south. The Israelis had bombed them under the pretext that they were Palestinians. We also passed the place that was the scene of the air raid I spoke of earlier. Several blocks along the sea were flattened and a family of ten were killed leaving one boy of eighteen alive. This area was under suspicion of bringing in arms from the sea for the Palestinians.

Journal Entry

Today we went to the vegetable market. Time has stopped here. We weave our way through the crowded street, passing stalls selling fruits, vegetables, fish, clothes, chickens with or without feathers, meat, singing birds, bread, garlic, and other spices. The smells are amazing and not very pleasant. There are many rotting vegetables and a sheep skin in a stinking pile, and beneath our feet there is mud and animal excrement mixed in. Yet, I look around me and I wonder at my presence here, and I look back to when my world was the size of Oregon.

Journal Entry

It is late at night; I am tired and go to bed. I am suddenly awakened by the thud and rattle of guns and my blood freezes. It stops after five minutes, and I go back to sleep.

Journal Entry

As a result of the air raid in the south, thousands of Palestinian refugees are pouring into Beirut with what belongings they have left piled on their heads. They make their way through the streets looking for empty apartments. Everyone carries something down to the smallest toddler. There are almost no men among them, they are either dead or have remained behind to protect what is left of their homes. As I look out the window, I see our street turn black with hundreds of people. They go from door to door asking for supplies and a place to live. People slam their doors in the faces of the refugees, and I wonder just who the enemy is. Later the Syrian soldiers go around with groups of people to each building and managers who have empty apartments are sometimes forced at gun point to let the people in. Everywhere there are people, cars and noise. So many people with nothing. I am humbled and thankful that I have been spared the agony of being homeless and hopeless. I merely have the acute feeling of being totally helpless to their plight. I think how stupid the people are to continue fighting and dying, and then I remember that it is not only they who continue. They are motivated, manipulated and supplied by the U.S.A. and Russia. The big men sit around their chess table and play at being God. The big men play, the innocent die, and it will be that way until there is no more greed and no more hate. Until there is a great silence on the earth and there is nothing but grass to cover our mistakes and nothing but air to tell of them.

Journal Entry

Now we are in the midst of the khamsin (meaning fifty), a hot dry dusty time with winds that blow for fifty days from the Sahara. Dust drifts on the balcony, we keep the windows tightly closed to keep out the dust and keep the coolness of the stone walls in.

Journal Entry

One evening as we are watching T.V., someone says it is raining. I hurry to retrieve my laundry from outside, and as I am reaching for the clothes the air explodes with sound; my head and body are compressed, my ears ring. I freeze for a second, then run for the shelter in the house. When no more bombs fall for a while I continue to get my clothes as it is still raining.

Journal Entry

Today we are inundated by the close sounds of machine gun fire and rockets. Two streets over and three blocks down is the dividing line between the Christian side of Beirut and our side, the Muslims. At this line there are Syrian guards who are now battling the Christian militia. It all began, I am told, because of a Foosball game between a Christian and a Muslim. The Christian believed that he was cheated and the two got in a fight. The Muslim wounded the Christian. In retaliation a sniper from the Christian side shot fifteen Muslims. The Muslims told the Syrians they must try to stop the sniper before the Muslims do. The Syrians warn the Christians to stop their sniper, or the Syrians will move inside the Christian area and take up positions to deal with anyone carrying a gun. When they began to move in, the Christians opened fire and now the Christians and Syrians are fighting each other. The air is reverberating with the thunder of heavy artillery; the windows rattle and I can feel the vibration in the floor.

Journal Entry

All the windows are open to avoid pressure breakage. I do not feel frightened, probably because it won't do any good, and because one gets a fatalistic attitude. I just go about my business of trying to survive. The bombs fall for a while and then a strange silence ensues as the forces change their positions. It all begins again from a different quarter. The bombs fall, the machine guns rattle, and the ambulance sirens follow. I am confused about some of the people's actions in this. The fighting is just two streets over, yet they go out in the street and talk. They stand on rooftops and balconies to watch. They let their children go off to school and play in the street. Being fatalistic is one thing, but gambling with the lives of the children is insane. The main difference on the street is the lack of cars. The usual bustling honking confusion is limited to school buses and public conveyances. I think about the people who will die today, and each one is Mohammed and a Christ. Their lives are given in vain, just as the great prophets before them. They speak meaningful words, yet the words and the wisdom disappear when the guns come out. All that is left is the sacrifice without the meaning or the honor. The innocent die without reason and the wicked hunt them without mercy.

Journal Entry: Christmas 1978

Our voices were drowned by the spatter of machine gun fire very close at hand from the opposite balcony, and every now and then the windows would rattle with the explosions from dynamite. When I ask if there is any danger, I am told "they are only celebrating" - blowing up things and shooting guns because of the war so newly finished. It used to be, they tell me, that all the downtown was brightly lit and decorated both for Christmas and New Years, and people would walk the streets wearing party hats, blowing horns, and having a good time until the morning. But now the guns fire and the wrecked cars explode, and everyone prays that someone will not get too upset and take revenge for something obscure and start everything all over again. The people are still nervous and volatile, arguments go on about nothing, usually ending up in a fight.

Journal Entry: April 1978

I attend my first Arabic wedding and find it a very enlightening experience. There are so many people and loud music and flowers. The bride wears white and is overly made up. She is so young and looks a little frightened. So often, the young people are married to people they hardly know. The mother of the bride is a formidable creature, big and loud, wearing the same black dress she probably wears to funerals. Drinks are passed around, alcohol to the men, orange juice to the women. The party grows in sound and people until well after midnight when the exhausted couple depart amid the sound of something resembling a war cry. In the middle of all this tumult it suddenly hits me that here I am, an American at a wedding full of people I don't know, for a couple I don't know, sitting around listening to a language I hardly understand, with my parents in-law that I could speak very little to, hearing music and seeing dancing that was all new to me. The funny thing about it is, I enjoyed myself thoroughly. Before this, the picture I had of the people as a whole was one of stubbornness and grim determination and an easily fired temper. But now I see another side, a very loving and happy people who know how to enjoy themselves when they can. Such things as weddings, births and deaths are very important parts of their lives, and each occurrence is given the attention it deserves.

Journal Entry: June 1978

Today we went on a picnic to Baalbek, historic Roman ruins of the temple of Bacchus in Lebanon. As we travel the winding mountain roads we went in and out of the Christian areas. At each checkpoint I pray they will not ask for our papers. We went steadily up from sea level to 4,000 feet in about half an hour. Then we began to descend into the Beqaa Valley, the richest-growing land in Lebanon. To the right was Mt. Hermon, at the top of which is the border between Lebanon and Israel. To the left is the highest mountain in Lebanon standing at 11,000 feet. Below us the valley is perfectly flat with squares of green in varying shades over its entire surface. Every nook and cranny is used to full advantage. We pass workers in the fields with hand tools and men tilling the soil with a wooden plow and mule. We pass shepherds with their flocks and a man walking beside a mule on which his wife and various provisions perch.

We arrive in the town of Baalbek: winding old streets, tree shaded in some places, glaring hot in others. On our left the temple comes into view. Colossal pillars rising out of the plains. Closer we come until we stop in the shade of its height. We walk up the great marble steps to the main entrance and are dwarfed by the great pieces that are so massive and ornately carved. They seem much too heavy to set atop a pillar. As we ramble through the place, I hear the ghostly sounds of marching feet and rustling togas and from the dungeons, echoes of doom. Under the palace is an underground archway running off in many directions. Here I imagine I hear the stamp of horses and the clash of sword and saber. We walk around and up and down until we are hot and tired and I feel I am just another dusty Roman looking forward to a little village fare.

Journal Entry: July 1978

The on again, off again, war is once more in the "on" position and the bombs leave their fiery tails across the night sky and their acrid smell in the balmy air. We stand on the roof top and gaze across the narrow valley to the facing hillside covered with buildings. The flash and echo of the bombs reach us minutes after the act has taken place. Someone laughs and comments on the marksmanship, but I cannot laugh, and I leave the rooftop because I know at the end of that blazing red trail there is an explosion that may totally devastate someone's life, I cannot laugh or enjoy the spectacle, I only want to weep for this fragile entity called "man."

It is early evening, and our guests are sitting on the balcony enjoying the cool breeze. I am in the kitchen preparing tea when suddenly my body and facilities were robbed of their function by a sound so huge I couldn't take it in. I stood numb, seconds later, I think "a bomb has hit our building", more seconds later "what of our baby asleep in her room", more seconds later "what of the people on the balcony?" My body somehow carries itself to the baby's room. It is filled with smoke and dust. The baby lays still in her bed. I run to her and grab her up and shake her. She was only sleeping, she was unharmed. The noise had been so enormous I couldn't believe she had slept through it. Finally, the confusion subsides, everyone is alright. We survey the damage and find that one large window not fifteen feet from the baby's bed is completely shattered. We step through the glass and peer out, to discover that three feet below the window is a hole half a foot across. The bomb had entered the apartment below us, tearing its way through three rooms demolishing almost everything. Fortunately, no one was at home.

Journal Entry:

We are sitting on the balcony watching the bullets and rockets whistle by three streets over, I cringe at every sound. But I am most horrified by the sounds of rockets. They burst from their launchers and rip through the air. It seems the air itself is screaming with agony. From what source did the minds come that conceived such atrocities, such mechanisms that eat away at the enemy and eat away at the heart and mind of the one holding the gun.

Journal Entry:

Humanity is doomed. This poor country has been violated too many times and she is empty and eaten away like so many of her buildings. The bombs fall and my husband puts arms around me and says "I'll protect you" and I look at him and hold him close because we both know there is no protection for any of us anymore. We are caught up in a spiral of the damned in which all of humanity will lose.

Journal Entry: July 4, 1978

The bombardment has continued since last night. I am completely wakeful holding my baby to me as we huddle in the corridor. The building shudders with the percussions of nearby bombs, the sweat standing on me, yet I feel no fear. I merely feel that fate will take care of the outcome. The only real fear I have is for my baby, whose small life has nothing to do with hate and war and I feel guilty for bringing her into this. Last night beneath the window I heard a soldier's heavy boots upon the pavement and the snap of machine gun clips being loaded. I wondered if he was crouched in the lee of our building, as I heard the spit of his gun so close and loud. I hoped there would not be retaliation. During the evening, we watch T.V. with the volume way up to drown out the noise. Later while waiting to fall asleep, I read yet I can't concentrate and gave it up. I turn out the light and stare at the ceiling and think about my husband, away on a trip. Tonight, will be as last night. I wonder how it will end.

Journal Entry: August 4, 1978

Today as usual the bombs and guns are sounding. The noise is usually in the distance but suddenly, we hear a loud report coming from the street. The story is that a young man from our building was being pursued in a car by the brother of a girl this young man had been irritating. When the boy got inside the building the manager locked the main door so that the man with a gun could not get to his quarry. So out of anger and the need to take revenge for his sister, The man with the gun shot the boy's car full of holes. One of the shots ricocheted off the pavement and hit a woman across the street in the stomach. She had just given birth to a child the month before. If she dies, her husband will undoubtedly go gunning for her murderer. There seems no end to it, revenge for revenge, hate for hate, killing for killing, and always the innocent falling to mark the advancement of stupidity.

Journal Entry: August 6, 1978

It is the second night of Ramadan, the Muslim's month of fasting. We sleep in the corridor again because of the bombs falling in our vicinity. The noise is so loud followed by irregular and long periods of silence through which I wait tensely for the next bomb to fall. I cannot sleep, neither can my husband. We hardly speak, just touch each other and our baby and wait. At 3:00 am the loud beating of drum echoes off the surrounding buildings. A man beats a drum and sings a song to wake the people who are fasting so that they may eat before the sun comes up on another fasting day. At 4:00 am the chanting from the mosque begins and so does another day and still we have not slept. I wonder what tonight will bring.

Journal Entry:

It is the third day of Ramadan and a young man of 25, a guard for the Parliament, was shot by a Christian sniper. He went to work at 8:00 AM and came home at 2:00 PM in a wooden box. The wailing of his mother and family is in the air and then come the long hours of the reading of the Koran over a loudspeaker. In what kind of life do we find ourselves? The bombs still fall.

Journal Entry:

It is the fourth day of Ramadan, and the young man is now on his way to be buried, compliments of the government. As he goes there is a deafening salute of machine-gun fire. He died by the gun, and he is buried by the gun. How I would hate such a tribute.

Journal Entry:

It is the fifth day of Ramadan, and an ambulance comes bringing the body of the woman across the street who was shot accidentally four days ago. She leaves a month-old baby, and her husband is an emotional wreck. He is thinking of revenge now and who knows what that will bring.

Journal Entry:

It is the seventh day of Ramadan we are reading our newspapers when the air explodes with machine gun fire from the street. It gets louder and louder and I run for cover. It's another funeral procession bringing back another victim of the sniper. We find later that another man died due to the "funeral announcement." He died in the street. People are dying right and left from stupidity. It's unbelievable.

Journal Entry:

It is the eighth day of Ramadan and the city echoes with endless funeral chants. When will it end?

Journal Entry:

A ten-story building was blown apart on the tenth day of Ramadan. The building contained the offices of the P.L.O. and some of its members. The building was blown up with many kilos of dynamite. It killed over 200 people and the person that was the target of the blast wasn't even there.

Journal Entry:

The night is a peaceful one and we sleep well, when we're awakened by a sound we can't place at first. We cling together as we realize it is the sound of Israeli bombers. The planes roar down, there is a whistle and a blast and the plane roars away again. There seems no end to this madness.

Journal Entry: September 27, 1978

It is late night, I am wakeful due to the now familiar "night thunder" I have completely lost track of reasons and sides and days, the fighting continues whether I understand it or not. Because the news is so confusing and because it troubles me, I make little effort to delve very deeply into the issues. My main concerns are keeping things that the baby needs well stocked in the house and making as few trips out as possible. I am learning not to react so violently to the deafening explosions and the ripping, tearing sounds of rockets. My baby clings to me when she hears these sounds, and she is only one year old. Why must she learn such fear, so young? It is so strange to sit here calmly writing while the bombs are falling outside. I suppose a person adopts a fatalistic attitude and goes about their daily lives. If I am to die, it may be today or tomorrow by gun, or bomb or car or sickness all I ask is if a bomb is to fall here and annihilate all that I know and love, please God do not spare me. I have this fear that I will be the only one left and that far outweighs the fear of dying.

Journal Entry:

The past two or three days, another sniper has been taking random shots at people on the street up from us. I cannot fathom the type of person who can, without feeling, kill old women going to market, young men and women going to school, babies and their mothers. To sit and take aim and fire as if that act would solve some world problem or political wrong.

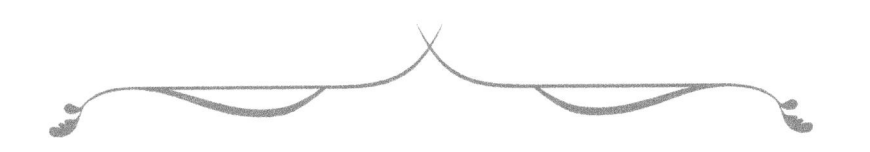

*Amid the rubble
the sniper waits
for his hatred to congeal
into a man.
He pulls the trigger
and watches his image fall
but he does not cry.*

Journal Entry:

We move to the protection of the corridor and the noise is absolutely horrendous. I sit rather numbly waiting for something I try not to imagine. The firing goes on into the night again. We all fear for tomorrow.

Journal Entry:

The guns sound, the rockets and mortars roar over our heads. The big men sit and talk, their smiles and their handshakes are filled with hypocrisy. The talk and we huddle in fear, the night drags on, and we are sleepless and afraid.

Journal Entry:

Today I see a beggar in the street, ragged and dirty. He carries a plastic bag and holds out his hand as he shuffles along. In the space of one block, seven people give him money or something to eat. Three children give him bread. One gives him a piece of candy. A tall soldier in his Khaki uniform bends down to the old man and gives him money. I am deeply touched by the kindness that I see, and it confuses me more than ever about this country. The picture of the soldier caring for the beggar is such a paradox. I am confused by the divergence of feelings among the people and in myself from my own observations. I feel hate for those that cause the bombs to fall. I feel love for mankind, I feel pain for this poor country and her beauty gone asunder, for its people gone astray, for its flag forever at half-mast. Where is the once proud Lebanon?

Among the rubble there lie pieces of pride, of loyalty, of beauty, of history. All that is left intact is fear and from that fear comes a new insane sort of loyalty, loyalty with the sense gone out of it.

Journal Entry:

Another day passes and my mind whips on and on trying to remember my feelings. I wish I had a tape recorder in my brain. that would record my thoughts continually, for what I have put down on paper is but a fragment of what could be said, and my mind is so hampered by the slowness of my hand.

Journal Entry:

Remembering the magnitude of sound is like remembering pain. The condition surrounding the noise or pain can be remembered but the essence of the effect escapes. We cannot recall the effect in its entirety unless we hear it again and then we can say "yes it was like that before" because we know that it is true.

Journal Entry: October 4th, 1978

Sunset comes quickly and the orange glow is diffused by the smoke of many fires. The sky is not visible, not even the tops of some nearby buildings. East Beirut is in flames in many places due to the fighting and yet it still goes on. The murky light deepens into night, a dark that has a texture to it. There are not many lights to be seen, most people have locked up their homes and gone away. All the streets are deserted, the smoke, the bombs, the eerie light gives me a lonely feeling I cannot describe or wholly accept.

Journal Entry:

During the night the soot falls like black snow, and everything inside and out is covered with a fine black film. The smoke and soot from the fires in Beirut reach beyond the Israeli border 30 kilometers away.

Journal Entry: November 1, 1978

Once more my baby and I huddle in the corridor, this time due to our own private neighborhood war. On the street level of our building is an office of the political group Amal. They, like all the other government offshoots, believe they have the last word in law enforcement. They all carry guns. They believe their cause is just and in the name of Lebanon. They caught a man speeding by their office and check point, so they shoot the tires to stop him. They got him from the car and questioned him. The man refused to admit to speeding. After an argument they shot him in the head. Now there are guns on every rooftop and all the shops are closed. The retaliation comes and we are inundated with sound and then it is over. These same "benefactors" of Lebanon beat a man to a pulp in front of the neighborhood children because they suspected him of having drugs.

Journal Entry: November 2, 1978

Now there are tanks below our windows, the streets are blocked, we are trapped. Machine guns, RPGs and bombs. It's the war all over again, but this time we are in the middle of it. I don't know what it's about.

Journal Entry: June 1979

All afternoon the Israeli jets go back and forth across the city, lower and lower, dropping bombs on the port of Sidon and points South. I hear the high-pitched engines in the distance, it becomes a roar as the race overhead and as they go, each outpost on the ground fires up at them with guns and antiaircraft missiles. Just as the noise builds up, it recedes again until they sweep back on the return from the sea. The streets empty as the planes come and refill as they go and I feel cold inside. During the night I lay awake and count the countless time, and I try to be calm to protect the new life that grows within me. Yet, as each bomb falls that life that knows no life reacts just as I do, and we cannot comfort each other.

Journal Entry:

The planes come again, the pattern repeats itself, and when it is over I go about my work feeling less enthusiastic and hopeful every day.

Journal Entry: June 16, 1979

All night the bombs fall with horrible regularity and all thoughts of sleep are abandoned. As usual I am unaware of who is fighting or for what reason.

Journal Entry:

Another sleepless night. At 4:00 AM everything suddenly becomes quiet, and we fall thankfully into exhausted sleep.

*Bombs fell continuously
around our hiding place,
our voices were lost
as was our hope.
Day and night and into time
we traveled through our Hell,
until at last without warning
we were cast adrift
in that strange shadow of sound;*

silence.

Journal Entry: June 18, 1979

The guns stopped firing because the army has come in and supposedly put a stop to everything. Streets that were barricaded are now open. There is dancing in the streets. As long as the army holds its position between the Muslims and the Christians, things will remain quiet. But how long is that?

Journal Entry: May 31, 1981

We decide to try to find an apartment in the mountains away from the troubled city of Beirut. We visit someone who lives there, and we soak up the silence and the peace. Evening edges down the mountainside reaching its darkening fingers into each tree lined gully and ravine. The sun lies just above the sea. It hangs there suspended for a moment before it slips into the sea. The evening enfolds me in deep purple and the lights of the city below begin to bloom one by one. It looks beautiful from up here, the twinkling lights belying security and peace. I sit upon this balcony over the valley like an eaglet in its eyrie, far above the poverty, the smell, the dust and the noise. Even the bombs make only the sound of distant thunder, Here the warm evening breeze brings the sweet smell of pine and scotch broom, birds twitter in the trees below. I left my fear behind me in that city, along with my innocence and my belief in the promise of humanity. It hardly seems fair to divorce myself so easily from the way of life there, when, to so many, that's the only life there is. I look up into the night sky, now covered by that ancient map of stars and I wonder at our frailty and our tarnished moment in time.

We find no places to live in the mountains. The drive back down the twisting roads is silent. The weight of fear returns.

Part III

BEIRUT AFTER THE SIEGE

February 1983 to November 1983

We left Lebanon and spent a year in Bangkok, Thailand. During this time, Lebanon was again the throes of war. The Israelis bomb and shell Lebanon from one side to the other. Beirut is under siege, no one can go in or out, all supply lines are cut off. There is no cooking gas, no water, no gasoline, no electricity. It's the same thing all over again, only the aggressor has changed. I feel guilty when I thank God that we are no longer there. So many people are dying. Somehow, I knew that something terrible would happen in Lebanon, more terrible than before. I felt such an urgency to leave, and people laughed when I voiced my fears of nowhere being safe in Lebanon. "The mountains are safe" they said, yet now Israeli soldiers are being dropped by parachute on those very hills and nothing is safe now. We worry about the welfare of my husband's family, and all we can do is watch the news and wait.

*Like mannequins
we wait
poised in still-life
for our fate.
We are weightless
and heavy with dread.
Others, our countrymen
lie timeless and dead.*

Journal Entry: February 1983

The siege of Beirut is over, we must return to Lebanon, once more to try to make our home. I am discouraged.

Journal Entry: March 15, 1983

Coming into the land mass of Lebanon we can see from the air the orange strings of streetlights winding along the coast road and into the city. After two years it is a sight of hope, there never were streetlights before. At the airport we are met by 15 armed men who search us before allowing us to go to the terminal. They are looking for drugs, as we just arrived from Bangkok.

Journal Entry:

After two years, much has changed yet it seems only yesterday we were here. It is bitterly cold, the coldest temperatures that Lebanon has ever known. In the mountains people and cars are disappearing under 12 feet of snow. In Beirut we are, as usual, without heat and electricity. During the day we wear 5 layers of clothing and during the night we sometimes sleep all together. When morning comes the last thing I want to do is get up. I work hard in the daytime to keep from being cold, my hands are cracked and occasionally bleed from the cold and the work. We go out in the car often as it's the only warm place. Home means nothing when it does not welcome you as a haven and a place of protection. The car seems more congenial than our home.

Journal Entry: April 8, 1983

    Today we get up early to go to a wake for a cousin of my husband, and the fiancé of his sister. He was just 23 years old, a lieutenant in the army, a leader of a tank battalion. They were ambushed and the tank in which he rode received a direct hit. He and three others were blown to bits, His remains were brought home in a sealed coffin that weighed almost nothing.

    As we drive along the coast road toward the south, we pass check points manned by the Lebanese Army, Italians and the Americans then by Israelis. One of them leers at me through the window of the car, I feel like a mouse under the eyes of a cat. On we drive through the battered remains of Damour, Sidon, and Tyre, and after 2 hours of jolting over roads scarred with 2-foot shell holes, we arrive in Nabatieh. All around, the flowers of spring are glowing in the sun, the grass green and luxuriant, cradling newly plowed earth. The scent of orange blossoms is in the air and even the mangled buildings are soothed by nature's caress. The house lies ahead, we are all deep in thought. I have not yet seen the way these people grieve, and I am nervous. As we walk up the porch we hear the wailing, my husband's steps slow, yet do not stop. Inside we find the mother curled fetus-like clutching a picture of her son and rocking back and forth. She says to the picture "My Son, My Son where are you? Are you hungry?" The relatives all begin to weep and wail, my husband tears his hair. I cannot afford to weep, and I offer my sympathy with silence. As the day wears on, more and more people come, dressed in black. They hug each other and weep and rock. The pain is deep. We all go to the graveyard where the black-clothed people look like crows among the white gravestones. At last, we stop at the grave. The wailing becomes awesome. They are terrified by their loss, and

I am terrified by their fear. On the way home the car is quiet, the same scenes roll by the window in reverse. Our days feel short.

Journal Entry: April 16, 1983

The American Embassy was blown up today. The seven-story building folded up into a pile. People were blown to bits, an arm here, a recognizable face there. One man was identified by the tailor who made his suit.

Bodies were blown into the ocean, others were buried under the rubble, some are missing altogether. Many Americans were killed, yet more Lebanese, those seeking visas and those working inside. No one knows who did it. or why, but it benefits many political groups who can use it for their various causes. I am greatly saddened.

Journal Entry:

Today a big plane came and took away the remains of the Americans killed in the Embassy. They have an army sendoff at the airport. Still all the love of relatives, all the care taken cannot bring back a life, nor mend the waste. When we shed our tears, I am not sure if they are for those who have died or those of us who are left to bear the pain of loss and the agony of our jumbled, pointless lives.

Journal Entry:

Today I walk on the beach outside Beirut, to the south beyond the Marine's check point. In the sea are many American destroyers, there is a landing stage not far from where I stand. A wall of sandbags surrounds the supply depot, atop the barricade waves the American flag. I wonder if those men feel the way I do when I see it waving there, so out of place. The sand is littered with garbage, though there is less than before. When the sea comes up it leaves a space of sand clean and sparkling and unsullied as God intended it to be. So many things go through my head when I look at the sea, I almost become a part of it. The ashes of my sister are part of the sea – not this one, yet all seas are ceaseless and therefore comforting. I look at the newly washed sand and I think about my husband, gone away on his wings. He is always away and believes I exaggerate my descriptions of our time in his absence.

I have lived in Lebanon for so many years and today is the first day I have walked along its shore. What a pity that man can take something pure like the sea and the air and make it into something we dare not touch. To be deprived of the compassion of nature is a sin against God.

Journal Entry:

Another day at the beach, the wind is up and drifting over the garbage dump, the smell is defeating. Helicopters race back and forth from the American ships in the sea, the Marines are practicing their skills, back and forth, down and up. The noise is awesome, even the ocean can't compete. Our feet are coated with tar and oil. The sand and oil together make a gooey substance that clings like a second sole to our shoes. On the way to the beach, we go downtown where the ruined buildings stand row on row. But now in a repairable part of the city, streets in the bank district are being repaired. Scaffolding lines each side of each building for blocks, the sounds of jack hammers and other equipment gives a sense of hope rekindled and a glimmering seed of rebirth.

Journal Entry: May 17

Today after many months of fruitless talks between the Israelis and the Lebanese, they agree to end the state of war between them. With the signing of this agreement, Lebanon has fallen to her knees, a proud but crippled nation.

Her boundaries are broken on one side, threatened on the other. She is forced to stand as a buffer between Israelis and American power, between Syrian and Russian might. And while she makes this sacrifice she is not praised, but forced to accept without a murmur the sealing of her doom. And the people of Lebanon, what of them? They go on as before, they buy, they sell, eat and sleep, are born and die, and when a child is born, they wonder to what has he been brought and when they die, for what have they lived? Without the pride of being Lebanese the people cannot fight back, and slowly the pride and loyalty will fade as the boundaries shift and change until one day Lebanon will cease, and like Atlantis, disappear.

Journal Entry: May 22

It's Sunday, the streets of our area are quiet, few cars are about. We drive toward the sea, and as the beach comes into view, it seems black with the masses of humanity that have crammed themselves onto a small stretch of fairly safe beach. The streets bordering the ocean look like 2-way parking lots, the cars just inching along. Their occupants staring at the occupants of other cars. The inhabitants of Beirut are trapped in an invisible cage of war. There are no bombs here now, no machine guns or rockets, yet the people are trapped. The mountains are inaccessible because of battles going on between the Druze Muslims and the Christians, The Beqaa valley beyond the mountains is under the influence of the Syrians. The Israelis control everything from Sidon

South. So the people of Beirut, a city of several million are confined to a small stretch of beach front, a small stretch of road with a view.

Up and back, up and back they go. The restaurants are too crowded and dirty to walk into. On all the faces there is the look of uncertainty and extreme boredom.

Journal Entry:

The night is troubled by the distant sound of bombs up in the mountains. They say it is between the Druze Muslims and the Christians. We fear that these two parties were put on their present course by the Israelis and the Syrians.

Journal Entry:

Today the news is grim. It is once again Sunday. The roads, the beaches and the arcades are crowded with people who want to forget. Out at sea are 10 American destroyers braced against the tide, there were only six ships before. No one knows what will happen next, though it is expected that war will come between Israel and Syria based in the Beqaa valley. Here in Beirut, it is said we will be untouched, yet the battles will rage around us, the airspace and borders with Israel and Syria will be closed. We again stock our cupboards and freezers hoping against the odds that someday that meaningless and nebulous word "Peace" will prevail. We drive by the area that used to be the American Embassy. So neatly it was carved from between three other connecting buildings. It is so obviously a professional job. I get so tired of trying to see reason where there is none, and stability where there is no hope of it. We have been married for almost eleven years and I have yet to feel settled.

Journal Entry: June 3, 1983

4:00 AM this morning we are torn from our sleep by a shuddering of the earth. The room is tossed side to side, things crash from shelves. Outside in other apartments people shout and run down the stairs. Out in the street a man shouts, "God help us!!" The tremors cease, the earth we live on is once more stable, but for a moment we were held in God's hand and were shaken to awaken our sense of proportion, our flimsy facade of human power that can be toppled in an instant by the will of God.

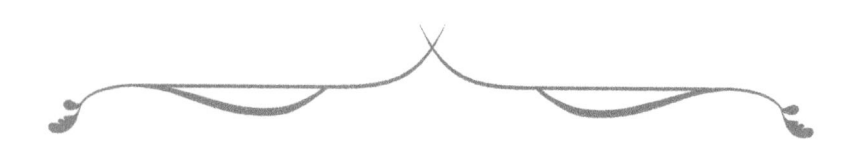

If there were hills to walk
I might find in that unpeopled space
a remnant of myself.
The scrap that once held smiles.

Journal Entry: June 6, 1983

It is one year today that the Israelis invaded Lebanon. The news shows films of the bombings and the murder. Babies were burned to death, or scarred by phosphorus bombs, old people were buried in their homes, hospitals were demolished, their patients unable to defend themselves or run. The shops are all closed today in remembrance, and it angers the Israelis who still control 30% of Lebanon and show no signs of going back where they belong.

Journal Entry:

Personnel carriers patrol the streets at all times of day and night, their rubber covered cleats cause a heavy rumble.

Journal Entry:

Every day there is an incidence of kidnapping or killing or bombing. Still the people watch with hope as buildings are built and streets are repaired, and lights go on where there were no lights before. Yet the future is dim, and the people see Lebanon shrinking to the size of Beirut.

Journal Entry: June 14, 1983

Parliament has decided to ratify the agreement with Israel, and Lebanon begins her decline in earnest.

Journal Entry: June 16, 1983

Israel has sealed off the south from Sidon on. Now, in order to get into that area, a person must get a card that is issued by the Israelis giving their permission.

Journal Entry: Aug 2, 1983

The rumble and clatter of tanks outside has caused us to go out on the balcony to see what is going on. We find our street blockaded by 2 tanks, several jeeps mounted with cannons and any number of armed men. They say they found a cache of weapons hidden in the basement of our building. People line balconies to watch, the soldiers warn them to go inside. The soldier's search reveals that a false wall was built in the office of the Red Crescent formerly located in the basement. Behind this false wall, boxes and boxes of all kinds of weapons were found. We have been sitting on top of a bomb.

Journal Entry: Aug 12, 1983

The airport is closed. It is being bombed from the mountains above, Lebanese against Lebanese. People are stranded. There was no warning of the closure or the bombings. The struggle becomes too much for me at times and I rely on fate to determine my course.

*My path has been determined
by a greater force.
It comforts me to leave
the future to that force.*

Journal Entry: Aug 29, 1983

The seven of us have been sitting for two days now, huddled in the corridor. Mattresses are spread on the floor between the corridor walls. I have such a sad feeling inside when I think of humanity. A mass of people made up of so many innocent souls who must bear the hatred borne by a few others who love the power of life or death. My children huddle against me. I want to weep, but I dare not. We were leaving here in two days, back home to Oregon where peace is as tangible as the grass. But no. The airport is closed. The news gets worse and worse. The terrible sounds of war get closer. It's amazing what humans can do to a beautiful day. My husband is not here, his plane was turned away from the airport.

Journal Entry: Barrage Day 3

The area is closed off by the political faction Amal who are against the rule of the Lebanese army. They decide that our area is a good place to fight the army and they place a cannon in the middle of our street. The street is cleared of cars. The Amal faction has taken up positions in all the entrances of all the buildings in our street. All is terribly, terribly silent. The afternoon wears on, clothed in a silent scream.

Journal Entry: Barrage Day 4

The barrage begins in the dark hours of morning as the tension increases, people begin to really fear for their lives. Many send their children to the shelter of the basement while the parents remain in their apartments. The shelter is dark and dank, lighted by one light bulb, the corners disappear into darkness. The air reeks of sewage and decay. The rats and cockroaches scurry about unseen but heard. I decline to send my children there, I feel in my heart if we are to die, it is better to be comfortable until that time. Time will answer the questions, and what I think and feel has no bearing on anything but myself and my children. I want them by me where I can hold them and tell them lies of safety.

Journal Entry: Barrage Day 5

We have been cloistered in the hallway now for 5 days. The days and nights are filled with incredible volume. I wonder how anyone can keep at such a thing as this for so long. The heavy mortars hit close to the building, some on the roof. The building quivers, and echoes of its anguish die slowly. I have drugged my children so that they might sleep the night away. I have more than enough fear for all of us. The morning comes, the barrage still goes on. Snipers are hidden on rooftops. The shots echo off and around the buildings so that the sniper's location is unknown. People are tired of not seeing the sky and creep out onto their balconies. It's a beautiful day. Purest blue sky. We humans tarnish the beauty of God. It is not possible that we were created in his image, for anyone so gifted as God, would be unable to create such an atrocity as man. As I write, shots whistle by the window. Fate compels me not to move.

The building has been given life,
it seems,
to view its own demise.
It shakes and shudders
as mortars fall upon the roof;
and echoes of its agony
fill our ears
with empty pain.

Journal Entry: Barrage Day 6

The night is silent, our ears ring with it. Dawn comes with a new round of fighting, to continue through the day, spaced occasionally by shreds of ominous silence. Standing on the balcony during a moment of quiet, I see the street stretching empty up and down, the dust and litter travel aimlessly. Above the street the tattered ribbons hang. They snap and turn in the wind, remnants of Ramadan

People are packing their cars and running away. Where they go, I don't know, as it seems every area has some fighting going on. Day by day the news gets worse, each morning I pray we live through the day and each night that we will see the morning.

Journal Entry: Barrage Day 7

The night passes in blessed peace, the morning comes laced with quiet and good news. The bombs have stopped falling, the trouble has moved on into the Beqaa Valley. In early morning light, even the buildings and the dirty deserted streets seem to breathe a sigh of relief. For several days and nights, we have lived hidden away in fear and now God has granted us this morning to once again view our lives from right side up. The streets are littered with the aftermath, broken windows and walls. On the upper street are a jeep and a tank, burned out, their occupants have remained inside until this day. As with all other aspects of life, some of us will grieve this morning while others will rejoice.

Journal Entry: Barrage Day 8

Our area is quiet though the bombs falling in the hills grow louder. A bomb falls in our area killing 10 people and wounding 45.

Our fear rekindles as the bombs get closer. It's been decided that I must leave our house. My husband is again away. I have put a few things in a bag for the children, and all the money and passports in my purse. My youngest sister-in-law comes with us. We clamber into the car and scared to death, I drive through the empty streets past the Amal checkpoints. Well-armed men stand ready, their faces covered with sack-like masks. The silent barren streets have an eerie dream-like quality. We finally arrive at the building of my husband's brother. He is not at home, and we cannot get into his house. The concierge shows us an empty apartment to use. It is very dirty, the windows are broken and there is no furniture but two iron beds without mattresses.

We cannot bear to stay in it, it's better to sit on the stairs. Finally, an empty office is located, we settle in with our blankets and pillows between the desks and papers, The children are delighted to play on the office chairs. The concierge brings us coffee, bread, cheese, and a radio. We wait out the night, the news is bad, the whole country is in an uproar.

Journal Entry: Barrage Day 9

The day comes again, it is the one reassuring thing that no enemy can take away. This area is now controlled by the army, therefore it is quiet. My husband's brother is missing, and my husband is out of Lebanon, but we don't know where. The concierge jimmies the lock of my brother-in-law's house.

Journal Entry: Barrage Day 10

The dark corridors of streets are silhouetted against the sky. Soulless windows are barren of light. We are now in the midst of our nightly plunge into darkness due to power cuts. Water is at a premium, and we fill the bathtub from a hose that snakes up the side of the building to a storage tank on the roof. This is utility water and used sparingly.

This segment of the conflict is beginning its 3rd week, we wait out the tedium of days by cleaning the house of our benefactor and spend the rest of the time in relative peace and quiet. The bombs can still be heard in the distance, though this area is an island of peace. People walk along the streets as before. We walk along the beach enjoying our freedom while others die in the battle zones not far away. How fickle life is and how fortunate we are to be able to see another day. There is a restlessness in me to be gone from this place and settle down to a peaceful existence. Yet, my heart goes out to this country, and I wish by my caring about it, its problems could be solved. But as always, through all of time a single voice is never heard. So, we wait in patient impatience to see if there is a tomorrow, and if there is one, to see what it will bring.

Journal Entry: Barrage Day 11

The war-torn city lies tumbled about me. Where has truth and beauty gone? Depression pulls me down in to the dark and sleeps with me in a night that never ends. Could it be that this is all there is? Is this my forever? The palm tree outside is dead. The dry rasp of its yellowed fronds is the only voice it has.

Wounds heal, however roughly. Time shows me how to cope. I look into this life to find the good things hidden away beneath the ruin. Every green leaf I see, every bird I hear is a miracle. Sun that flickers in the window is a direct caress from God. It is a message that tells me I am not forgotten. The smell of morning coffee, the shine of clean floors and windows. The splash of ocean waves upon the rocks of the coast. How they sparkle when the waves recede. Season changes show in the play of light and shadow. The rain falls like tears upon the pain this country holds. Yet, salvation is written in the air. One has to but notice they are alive, to be granted that final peace in death.

I watch a kite fly in blueness above the wasted city. Its wings are my wings. It carries me with joy beyond the everyday. When I truly "see" I am free.

Journal Entry: Barrage Day 12

We have been in our peaceful haven for 3 days now, bombs are heard in the distance, but our sleep is undisturbed, Still, the worry what is to become of us weighs heavily and the days stretch out, every hour a load to carry. My husband has finally contacted us, he will be coming by boat in two days from Cyprus. Our home area of Chiah has been under almost continual barrage since our departure, yet our apartment and contents are still undamaged. It is amazing how the brain endures such trials as bombs and fear and when it is free from those trials it forgets what has been, very like the pain of childbirth.

Journal Entry: October 6, 1983

More than a month has passed since the war began. We are still safe in our refuge, yet no stable solution to Lebanon's problems have been achieved. Winter has come to the mountains where people live in tents or schools or just under the sky. There is a shaky ceasefire that is continually being violated. Our area of Chiah is like a ghost town, all the people are gone. I'm scared to go to our house. The silence is ominous. There are masked gunmen in the street. Our neighbor across the street had a bomb in their house, windows broke all around, though ours are still intact. I want to make arrangements for the children and myself to go to the states. The future here is so uncertain. There are no schools opening, we cannot go to our home and our benefactor wants his house back. Our freedom to live a sane and normal existence depends on the availability of seats on an airplane. My patience wears thin.

But suddenly another unbelievable conflict arises.

Journal Entry:

"You can leave Lebanon if you want, but the children stay here." my husband said.

At that moment my heart stopped and started again, my future collapsed and reformed. In that moment my children became my only reason to exist. Their safety and their future far outweighed my own.

"I'm staying" I said.

Journal Entry:

The wind whips and whines around the house and through the windows. Winter is coming with a vengeance, and I think of those people without homes and adequate clothing. The wind blows stronger and in my mind, I hear the flapping and chattering of the refugees' tents in the wind.

Journal Entry:

I'm afraid my journal has lapsed these past few weeks, the frustration of going on day after day not knowing what the future will bring or what tomorrow will bring has defeated me. We have made and changed plans for leaving here so many times I cannot count them. The airport is open now and flights are fully booked for weeks, from here, from Cyprus, from London. Now we must leave our haven and go back to Chiah as the owner of this house wants it back. We pack our things and go.

As we approach our street the people thin out, the cars disappear, a silence hangs over everything. The electricity is off, we light our way up the stairs with a flashlight, our steps echo, nobody talks. It's night, the bombs and guns start again. It is as if we stepped across an invisible line that separates war from peace.

Journal Entry: October 23, 1983

The US Marines headquarters and a group of French paratroopers have been blown up almost simultaneously on a Sunday morning, 6:00 AM. No one knows who is responsible, but it is obviously some force that does not want peace in Lebanon. There is no peace really, anyway. I believe it is a pre-war rush. The streets are full of tanks, guard posts are everywhere. Trucks of armed men go here and there. It is quiet here in Chiah now, slowly life is trickling back into the area. But for how long?

Journal Entry: October 27, 1983

Finally, after umpteen delays and frustrations my children and I are leaving Beirut. The security at the airport is such that we cannot get close to the terminal but must drop our bags beyond a sand-bagged area. There is a tank parked outside, we must walk around it to get aboard. The bus stops before the plane. Everyone's bags are lined up by the stairs. We must claim them before we board.

Finally the plane takes off. I always felt that once we left Beirut, I would feel great relief. I am relieved, yet there I also feel an emptiness, a void, a great sadness for what has been, for what could have been, for what will never be. Lebanon is struggling with her last breath and for her and with her I grieve.

In my broken Arabic, I try to tell of the woe of the people in their own voice, to tell of the pain beneath the smiles.

LESH AMTIPKI?

Buddi ode bi jebbal
tat il shezerah,
woo shuf il bahar tahead.
Buddi shim il howa helway
mish il dachan min darub.
Darubna,
darubna,
kilinhar woo kililel.
Mowitna,
mowitna.
Haram ya baladi,
haram ya baladi,
buddi shuffic min zameen.

Translation:

WHY DO YOU CRY?

*I want to sit on the mountain
beneath a tree,
and watch the ocean below.
I want to smell sweet air,
not the smoke of bombs.
They bombed us,
they bombed us,
every day and every night.
They are killing us,
they are killing us.
My poor city,
My poor city,
I want to see you as before.*

Journal Entry:

Lebanon is dying, we see the descriptions of her gradual and agonizing demise every day in the newspaper. They say that Lebanon was a beautiful country before the wars began: colorful, culture laden, a symposium of people from everywhere, all contributing to the pattern of Lebanon's fabric. Now what is left of the fascinating cities, the ancient ruins, the orchards of orange and lemon? Ancient columns are toppled, contemporary structures twisted and broken, a mockery of modern civilization, an unsuitable tomb for so many, an ending of despair without a spark of hope, the mark of the end of faith, of trust, of human decency. And what of those who lived through the falling of the bombs, the collapse of buildings, the nightmare search for loved ones in improvised hospitals and morgues? We should hear their cries, no matter where we are in the world, their agony should be our agony, their fear, our fear.

For, if we do not feel with their plight and turn our faces away, then we are no better than the aggressor who dropped the bombs; for our blindness is the most powerful, more dangerous and more frightening than any weapon yet devised. The word: "concern" is becoming obsolete, the word: "humanitarianism" is gone.

Part IV

THE CLOSING DOOR

In 2005, the revolving doors of the airport swallowed up the form of my pilot husband of thirty-two years. He did not look back. Suddenly my life was uncontrolled. I cried. It surprised me that I still had tears left. As I drove away from the airport I realized that my now unformed life was full of possibilities. The thought was daunting and yet exhilarating.

I was fifty-five years old. Time to be reborn.

TWENTY YEARS ON

*You are but a figment now,
just a face floating out
of amorphic time
to haunt me with dreams
that once were all too real.
Wisps of memory
wind themselves
around and through
my sleeping heart,
to once again leave those invisible
wounds that never heal.*

EPILOGUE

It is 2024, and another war in Lebanon rages, chillingly similar to its past wars. I shudder in my freedom as I walk through peaceful streets that ring with the silent cries of other streets under siege. Birds do not sing on those streets. Quiet in a war zone is pressure-filled. I lived those past wars in person, I live this one in my soul.

The smell of fresh coffee lingers in the kitchen, breakfast leavings litter the countertop. I observe these things and feel guilt at the waste and the plenty, at the very idea of sitting down to a quiet breakfast. The shower water runs hot from the tap, it slips idly down the drain. I turn it off. I know well the lack of that precious commodity. The day passes, cars with full gas tanks come and go. The garbage truck comes to remove the evidence of waste from sight. Lights come on in the street as dusk falls, lights bloom in the houses. My bed calls me, yet sleep is fitful. The silence is a shadow of the remembered sound of war.

As I write the final pieces of this journal, I look back over all that has befallen me. I am so entirely grateful for my continued existence. There were times when there was no future in the offing, no glimmer of a life without fear and loss. Yet here I am. Miracles are possible. I have learned so much about myself through all of this. I have learned to embrace the simple, and to be aware of the movement of sunlight across the floor, of my breath flowing in and out. I have been delivered from the destruction of my soul. It makes me weep to realize that at this very moment forty years later things remain the same there. The bombs continue to fall, the innocents still perish. We as humans should be ashamed for all the inhumanity we have spawned. How can we say that we bless the hands of God while we desecrate his gifts to us, and massacre our own reflections? What will become of us? Will we lose our way in the dark?

The sky is blue today. The past and its pain are long departed. There are no bombs falling, there are no fault-finding in-laws. There are no deserted streets drifting with rubbish. My husband of this new life busies himself mowing the front pasture. My rescue horse munches happily in the paddock, the dog lies sprawled at my feet. In the fern bed, the cat hides, stalking birds at the feeder. My life hums contentedly to itself. Tears of joy and gratitude flow, replacing all those tears of woe and fear. The pain of years.

I have been a long time leaving.
Carol Hayes, 2024

Milton Keynes UK
Ingram Content Group UK Ltd.
UKHW042239011124
450424UK00001BA/82